Tell Me a Story

by Lili Henderson
illustrated by Lesley Breen Withrow

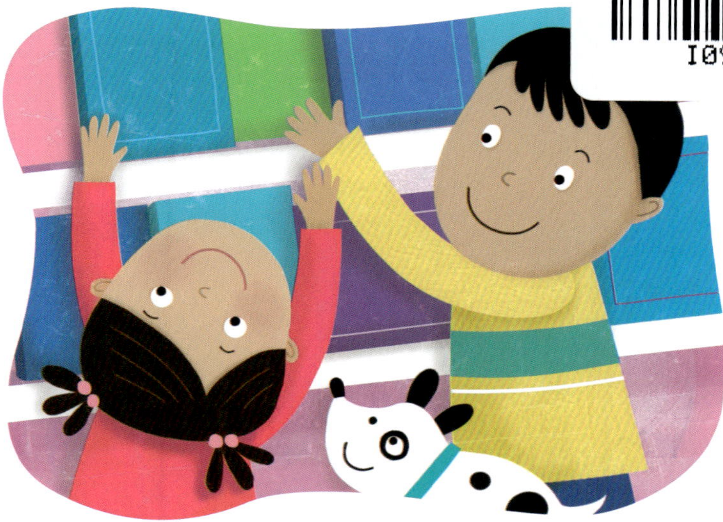

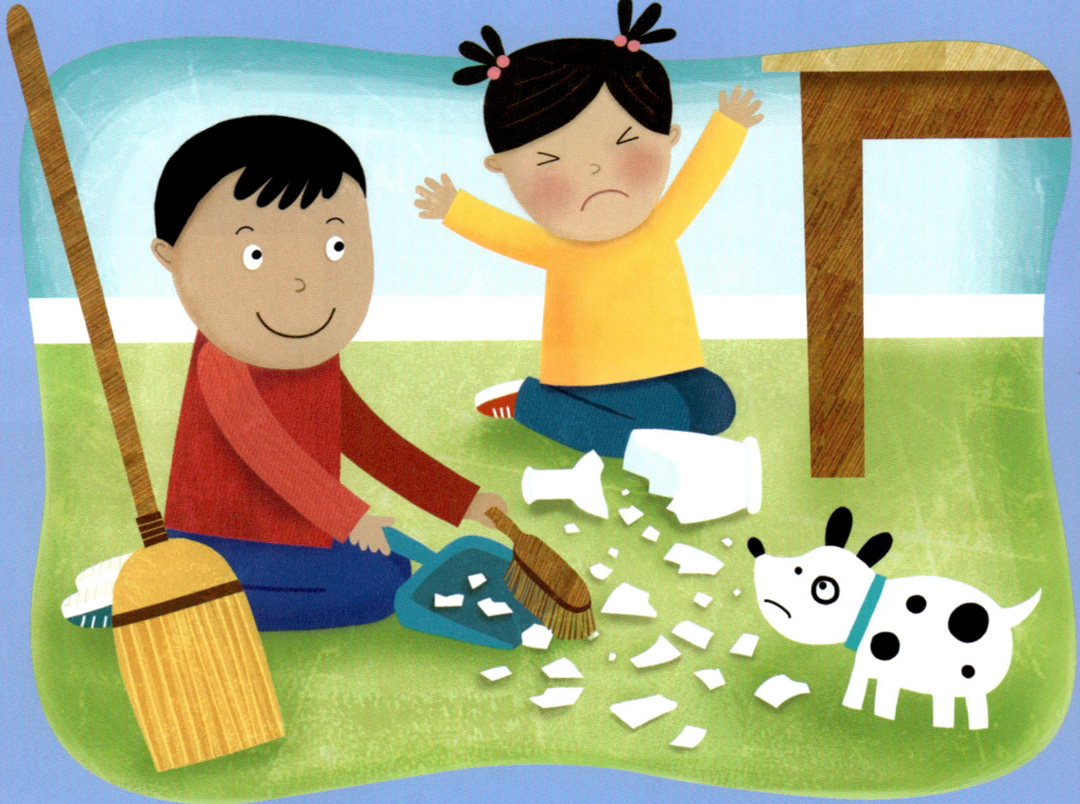

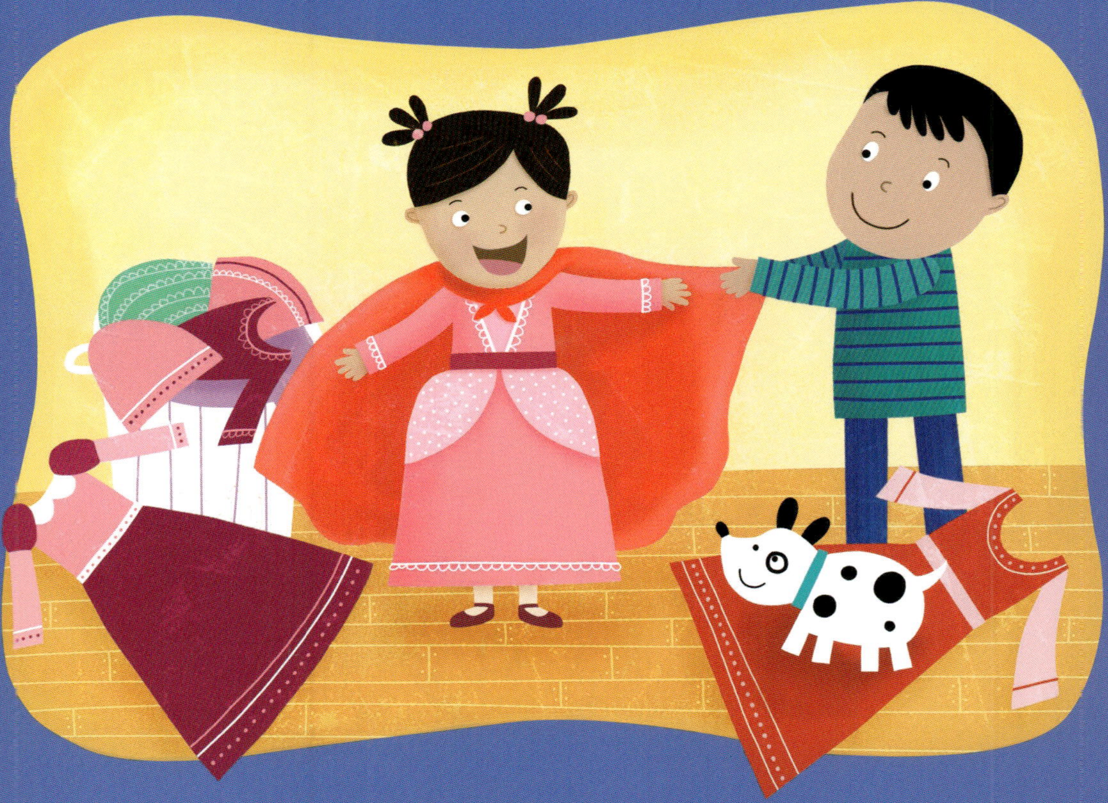

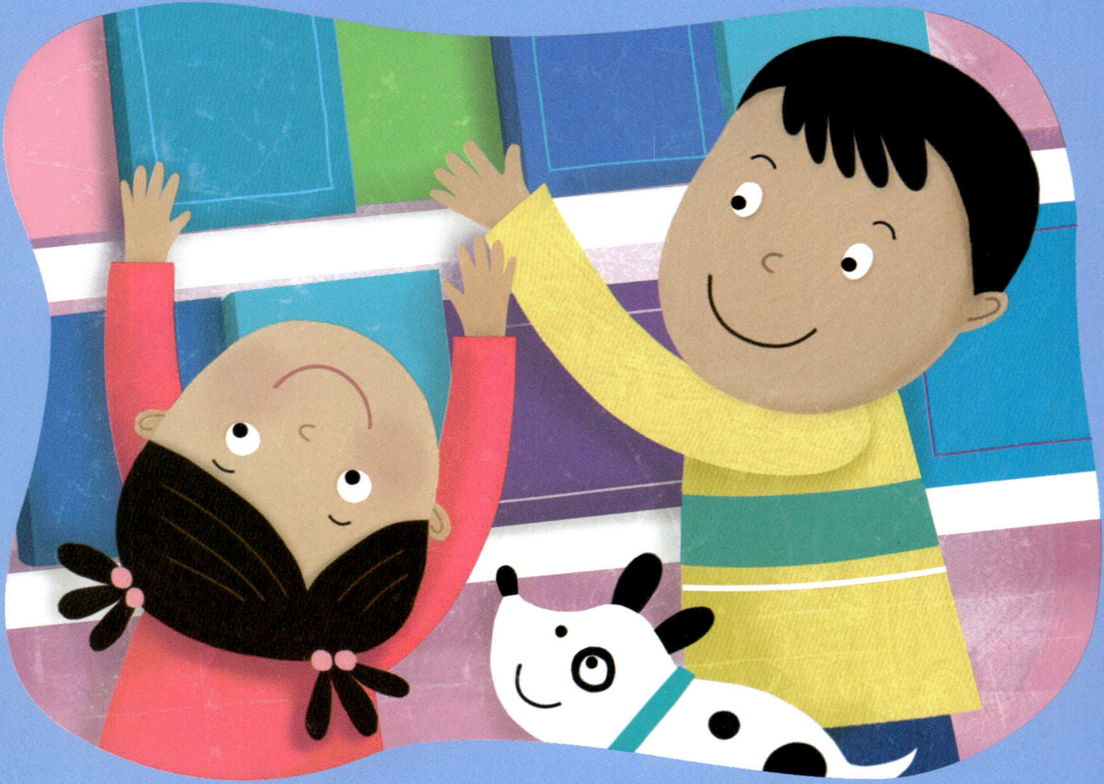

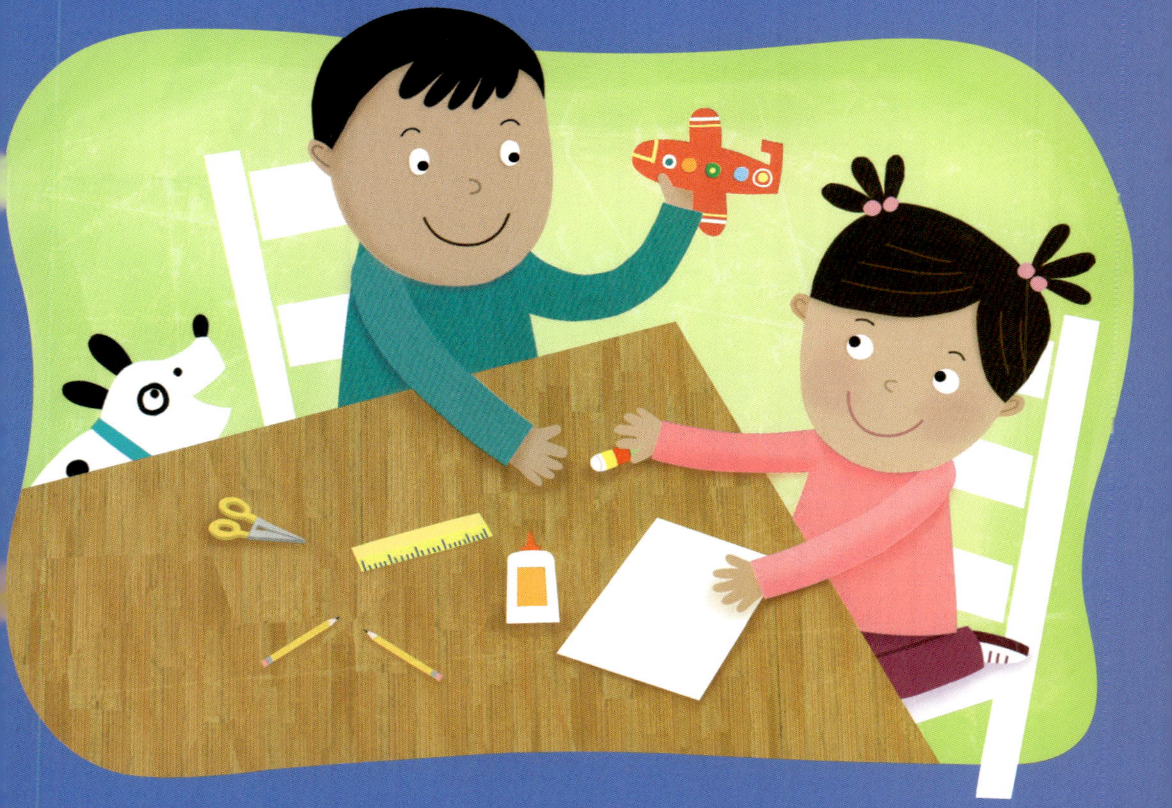

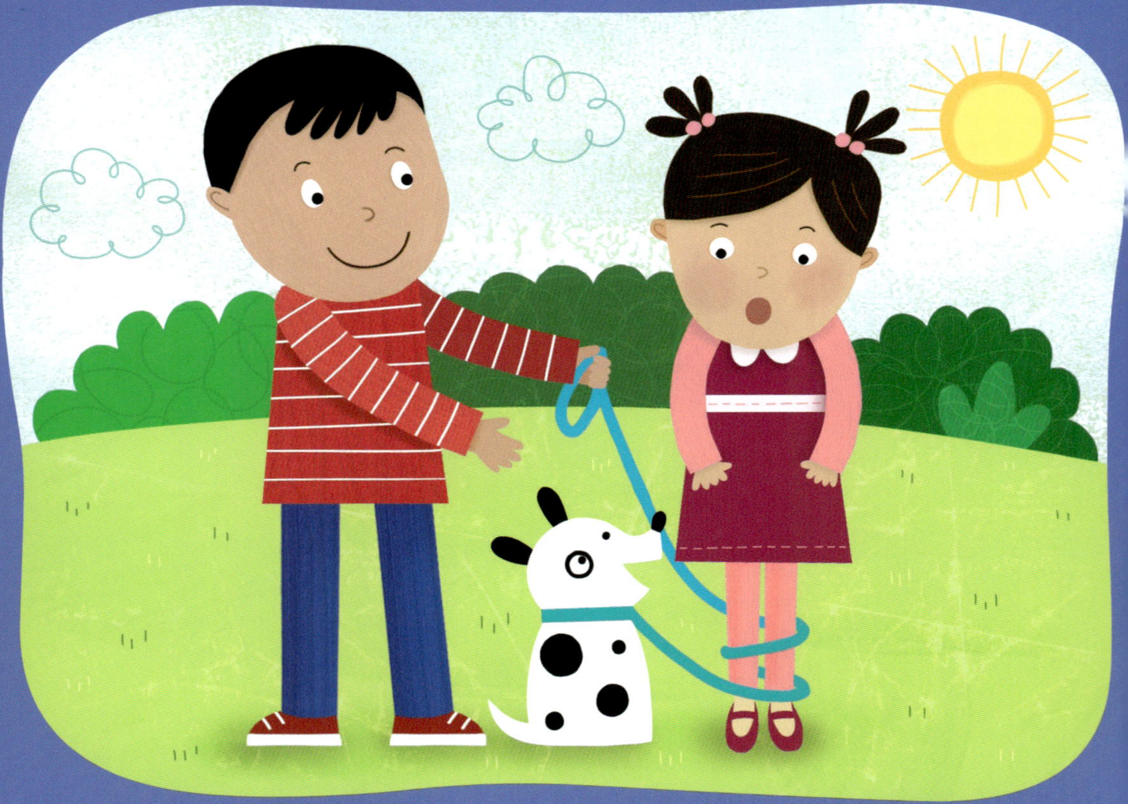

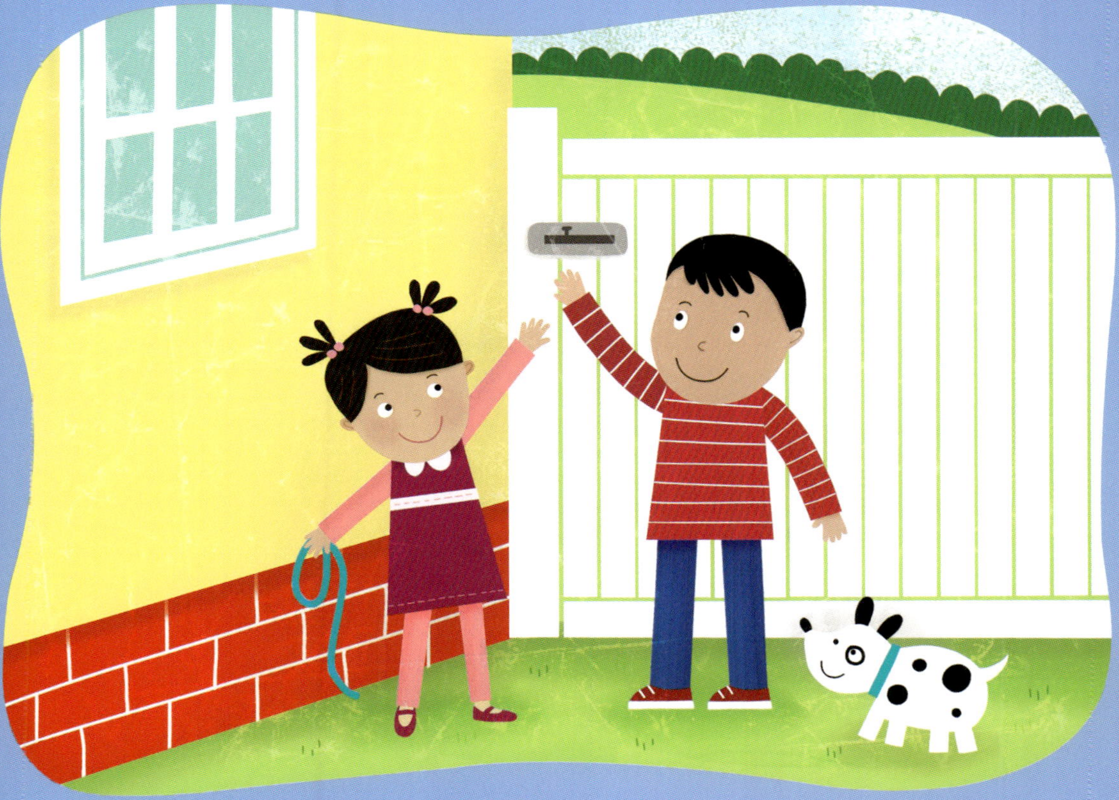

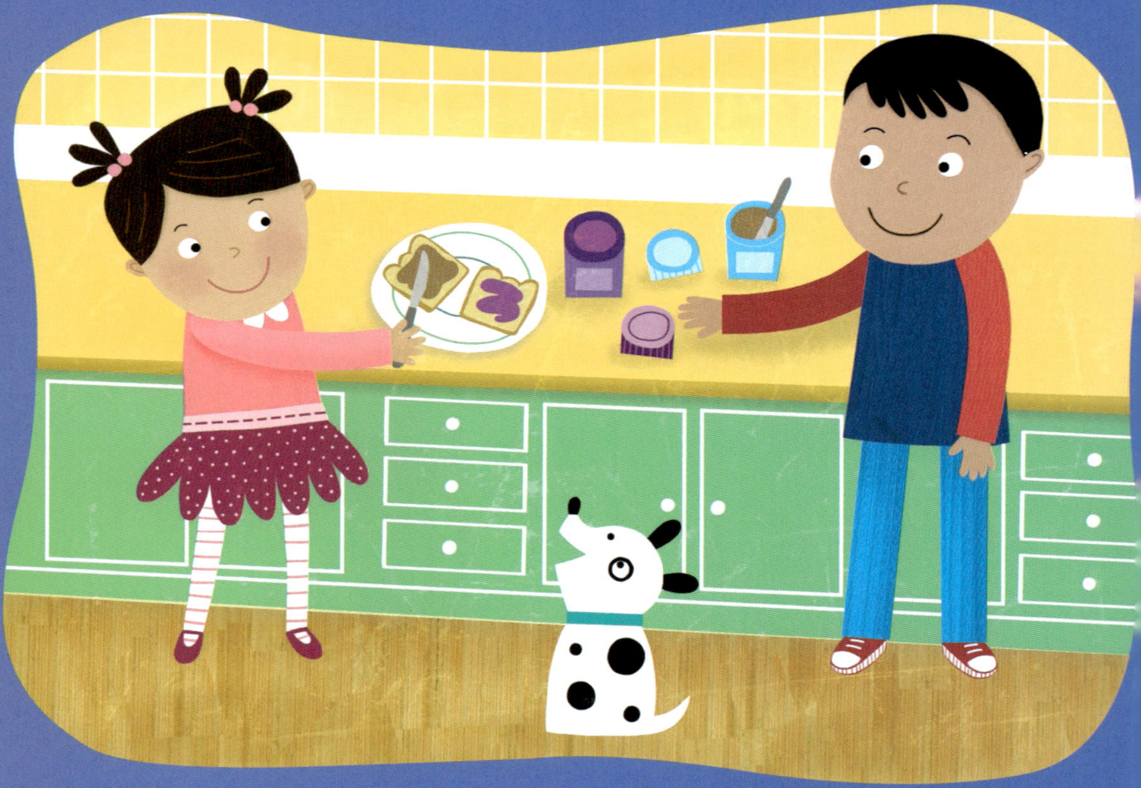